21st Century Skills Library

ANIMAL INVADERS

PYTHON

BARBARA A. SOMERVILL

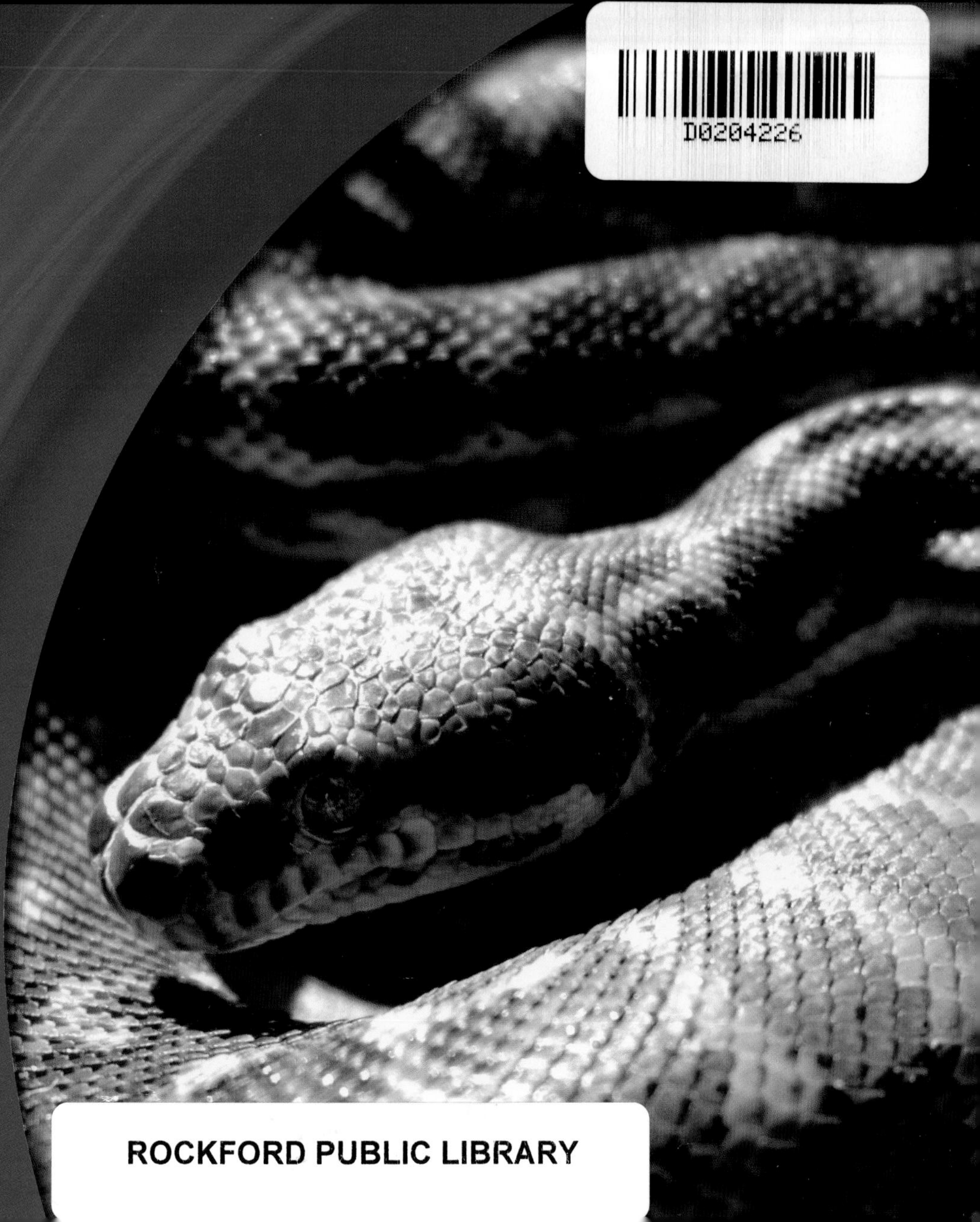

Published in the United States of America by
Cherry Lake Publishing, Ann Arbor, Michigan
www.cherrylakepublishing.com

Content Adviser
Dr. Sarah Simons, Executive Director, Global Invasive Species Programme

Credits
Photos: Cover and page 1, ©Sharyn Young, used under license from Shutterstock, Inc.; page 4, ©iStockphoto.com/poco_bw; page 7, ©wagtail, used under license from Shutterstock, Inc.; page 8, ©iStockphoto.com/Snowleopard1; page 10, ©Zanchika, used under license from Shutterstock, Inc.; page 12, ©Jeff Greenberg/Alamy; page 15, ©Joy Brown, used under license from Shutterstock, Inc.; page 16, ©Victor Soares, used under license from Shutterstock, Inc.; page 18, ©Bob Blanchard, used under license from Shutterstock, Inc.; page 21, ©ASSOCIATED PRESS; page 22, ©NatalieJean, used under license from Shutterstock, Inc.; page 24, ©Stevenoakes/Dreamstime.com; page 27, ©JJ Morales, used under license from Shutterstock, Inc.

Map by XNR Productions Inc.
Please note: Our map is as up-to-date as possible at the time of publication.

Library of Congress Cataloging-in-Publication Data
Somervill, Barbara A.
  Python / by Barbara A. Somervill.
    p. cm.—(Animal invaders)
  Includes bibliographical references and index.
  ISBN-13: 978-1-60279-629-4
  ISBN-10: 1-60279-629-7
  1. Pythons—Juvenile literature. I. Title. II. Series.
  QL666.067S66 2010
  597.96'78—dc22   2009026013

Cherry Lake Publishing would like to acknowledge
the work of The Partnership for 21st Century Skills.
Please visit *www.21stcenturyskills.org* for more information.

Printed in the United States of America
Corporate Graphics Inc.
January 2010
CLSP06

TABLE OF CONTENTS

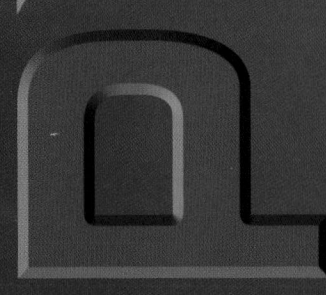

CHAPTER ONE
S·S·S·S·SNAKES!

A farmer is afraid. A snake is slithering on the grounds of his poultry farm in Miami-Dade County,

You don't want to come face-to-face with an African rock python.

Florida. Animal rescue workers arrive to find an amazing sight. It is a rare African rock python. The snake is 10 feet (3 meters) long and it has just swallowed a whole turkey. Its belly is bulging so much that it cannot slip back under the farmer's fence.

A golfer hits his ball into the high grassy rough along a Miami-area golf course. He knows better than to go after balls lost in the water traps. Alligators are in that water. But he didn't count on finding a 12-foot (3.7 m) Indian python coiled up and snoozing in the afternoon sun. Startled by the snake, the golfer runs to get help. It takes three strong men to capture the heavy reptile. One man grabs the head to control the python's fangs. The other two deal with the powerful body. The snake will be examined to make sure it is healthy. Then it will go to a reptile farm and become a tourist attraction.

A family visits Everglades National Park. They hope to see egrets, cranes, and wood storks. The sight that draws their attention, however, is quite different. An American alligator and a Burmese python are locked in one of nature's great wrestling matches. The snake has coiled itself around the alligator and is trying to squeeze it to death. The alligator has grabbed the snake in its mouth and is rolling toward the water. This is not the first such battle that Everglades visitors have witnessed. As the number of pythons in the Everglades increases, it won't be the last.

LEARNING & INNOVATION SKILLS

Dealing with Florida's python situation is complicated. Solving the problem will require a joint effort by teams of scientists from different organizations. Those organizations may include the Florida Museum of Natural History and the University of Florida. The Florida Fish and Wildlife **Conservation** Commission and the U.S. Geological Survey may also be involved. Before scientists come up with a way to handle pythons in the Everglades, they must learn more. They are asking important questions: How many pythons are in the wild in Florida? What do they eat? Where do they live? What other questions do you think need answering before scientists can solve southern Florida's python problem?

Pythons do not belong in the Everglades. And they are not the only unwanted creatures roaming the state. Florida has more than 200 animal and plant invaders, including parrots and climbing ferns. The state's warm climate is inviting for many **invasive species**. But the arrival of invaders such

Pythons and other invasive species have become a major problem for many Florida ecosystems.

as pythons has come at a price. They are squeezing the life out of the Everglades. This area is a delicate **ecosystem** struggling to survive.

CHAPTER TWO
ALL ABOUT PYTHONS

A python lies in the water with only its head peeping out. This **predator** waits for its next meal. A wood stork dips its beak into the water in search of food, and the python

Tree frogs make excellent snacks for pythons.

strikes. Its teeth sink into the stork's flesh. The python wraps its powerful coils around the bird and holds tight. Pythons do not produce venom, or poison. They do not crush their victims to death, either. They just squeeze tighter and tighter until the **prey** can no longer breathe. The victim **suffocates**.

After the prey dies, the python begins the long process of eating. Like most snakes, pythons eat their prey head first. The snake eats the stork whole—beak, feathers, bones, and all. The python is sluggish right after eating. It can take several days to digest a big meal. The snake may not need to eat again for weeks or even months.

Pythons are **nocturnal** predators. They hunt by ambush. This means they hide and attack by surprise. They use special heat-sensing areas in their heads to locate prey in the dark. Pythons are native to Africa and Asia. There, pythons prey on small animals such as ground squirrels, rats, and birds. They have also been known to hunt large prey such as leopards, antelopes, and deer.

Picture a female python as she curls around a nest of eggs. She is about 10 years old. This is her third group of eggs. Female pythons lay their eggs and then protect them from harm. Raccoons, foxes, and other animals raid bird and reptile nests for eggs. But most animals will steer clear of a nest protected by the jaws and coils of a mother python.

After mating, adult females lay between 20 and 100 eggs. Eggs hatch after 60 to 80 days. The mother goes without food for most of that time. She leaves the babies to care for themselves while she hunts for food. Pythons can hunt as soon as they hatch. Newborn pythons are 18 to 24 inches (45.7 to 61 centimeters) long. They grow quickly and double their length in a year.

Only a handful of pythons survive to become adults. Young pythons are eaten by birds of prey, certain mammals, other snakes, and even large frogs. Eagles, lions, and leopards hunt adult pythons.

Camouflage makes it easy for snakes to hide in their natural habitats.

21ST CENTURY CONTENT

How have invasive species become such a global issue? One way is through their ability to adapt easily to new homes. Pythons, for example, can fit in anywhere that the climate is reasonably warm. That includes southern Florida. Pythons are "**habitat** generalists." They can make their homes in wetlands, grasslands, or forests. They swim and climb trees. Pythons eat mammals, birds, and other reptiles. This means they can feed in most habitats. Can you think of more characteristics that help invaders such as pythons adjust to living in Florida?

Adult pythons have **camouflage** coloring. They are speckled with shades of brown, tan, and green. They blend in well with the undergrowth where they normally live.

According to the San Diego Zoo, there are 33 species of pythons. Burmese pythons are the most common pythons invading Florida. They grow to approximately 19 feet (5.8 m) long. They weigh up to approximately 200 pounds (90.7 kilograms). A healthy python in the wild can live up to 35 years.

CHAPTER THREE

HERE COME THE SNAKES!

O n any day, as many as 70 shipments of exotic animals arrive at Miami International Airport. Although some

Students in Miami, Florida, hold a python at an educational event.

species are legal, many are illegal. Some exotic animals are brought into the United States for zoos. Most are sold as pets.

People who live in the United States can legally own 22 different python species. The Burmese python is one of those species. Burmese python babies are sold for as little as $20.

Owning an exotic pet is trendy in Florida. Many people purchase pythons thinking they will be great pets. People are happy with their baby reptiles. But pythons don't stay babies for very long. Owners feed baby pythons a mouse once every couple of weeks. As the python grows, its appetite increases. By the time the python celebrates its first birthday, it is eating rabbits or whole chickens. It passes large amounts of solid waste. It needs a larger cage and is not as easy to handle. By this time, the snake has often become a nuisance for its owner.

Many python owners in southern Florida take their unwanted pets to the Everglades and release them. It may seem like a solution to the problem. The environment is one in which the snakes can thrive. All the pythons being released, however, are adults. There are no lions or leopards—and few eagles—to prey on the python population. Pythons have become top predators in the Everglades.

They are also breeding. Pythons start reproducing at about age 3. They continue to do so every 2 or 3 years for the next

20 to 25 years. Remember that few predators prey on pythons in the Everglades. This means it is likely that the survival rate will be higher than in the python's native homelands.

21ST CENTURY CONTENT

There is a safer way to get rid of unwanted pets than tossing them out in the Everglades. The Florida Fish and Wildlife Conservation Commission has a Nonnative Pet Amnesty Program. On special days, people can surrender their unwanted pythons and other nonnative pets to animal rescue agents. There is no charge, and the animals may be given to new owners. This event is expensive to run. But the program is much cheaper than dealing with major invasive species problems in federal and state parks and preserves.

It can be dangerous for untrained people to handle snakes.

CHAPTER FOUR
PROBLEMS WITH PYTHONS

Between 2002 and 2005, a total of 201 pythons were captured or found dead by Everglades National Park rangers. During the next 2 years, the number of pythons captured or found dead more than doubled to 418.

Pythons on roads are a big problem for many Florida drivers.

Just how many pythons are slithering through the Everglades? No one knows. And the pythons are not lining up to be counted. Everglades wildlife **biologist** Skip Snow estimates there may be more than 30,000. A general rule for snake counting is that you can usually find less than 10 percent of any snake population. Every 100 snakes found probably represents a population of 1,000 or more.

Since 2006, trackers have caught seven pregnant female pythons and one nest of eggs. One of those potential mothers carried 85 developing eggs.

In recent years, pythons have been on the move. As the **feral** python population increases, the snakes spread into new territories. They now live in Big Cypress National Preserve north of the Everglades and on Key Largo to the southeast. Many state and local parks, private property regions, and undeveloped land areas also house pythons.

Another problem with pythons is that they have become a serious traffic hazard. When dusk approaches, the snakes slip onto roads to soak up the heat held in the cement or asphalt. Imagine a driver's shock in discovering that the "speed bump" he just ran over is a snake as long as his car.

Most pythons die after being run over. Their bodies are studied, and they help scientists understand the scope of the python problem. Scientists **dissect** the dead pythons to find out what the snakes ate. The python's menu includes American alligators, raccoons, bobcats, white-tailed deer, rabbits, and gray squirrels. Those animals are plentiful in the Everglades. But they are also food for other native species. Panthers, bobcats, and alligators compete with pythons for food.

Wood storks, Key Largo woodrats, and other Florida **endangered** species have also been found in the bellies of dead pythons. For conservationists, this is serious. Florida's endangered species already struggle because of loss of

The wood stork is just one of the many species threatened by the presence of pythons in Florida.

habitat, pollution, and other factors. Now, they must battle another threat.

One problem endangered species face is that they have no experience with pythons. They do not know how to avoid becoming prey to these snakes. Many species teeter on the brink of extinction. They cannot survive if pythons prey on their struggling populations.

 **LIFE & CAREER SKILLS**

Scientists who study reptiles and amphibians, including snakes, are called herpetologists. Herpetologists work at universities, museums, and zoos. They also work at aquariums, reptile parks, and for government agencies. Experts worry about several of Florida's endangered or threatened snake species. Eastern indigo snakes, for example, suffer because of python competition for food and habitat. Herpetologists have teamed up with conservationists to study Florida's python problem. Working as a group is one of the best ways to find tools and strategies to help improve conditions. Why do you think that is?

In 2008, the U.S. Geological Survey (USGS) predicted that invasive pythons could easily spread throughout the South and as far west as California. They suggested that the pythons could easily live in the climate of these areas. But scientists did not say that pythons would definitely move so far. They simply said that it was possible. They stated that pythons have expanded in Florida and continue to spread.

This study was immediately followed by another that suggests that pythons will most likely remain in Florida. This was based on climate changes and drought conditions that might prevent pythons from straying far from southern Florida.

21ST CENTURY CONTENT

In 2009, Florida's governor has asked wildlife officials to begin trapping pythons. Florida's Congress is also considering planning organized snake hunts in the Everglades. Some Floridians worry that python hunting is coming too late to control the growing snake population.

Firefighters help a wildlife expert place a captured python in a container. The snake was pulled out of a drainage pipe.

Whether pythons spread beyond Florida's borders or not, the snakes are having an impact on the state. Studying, capturing, and removing pythons is expensive. Even worse is the impact on endangered species and the Everglades. That cannot be measured in dollars.

CHAPTER FIVE
STOPPING THE SPREAD OF SNAKES

In the city of Marathon, Florida, a meter reader for the water department watches for pythons. He is a member of the Python Patrol. Alison Higgins of the Nature Conservancy

The citizens of Florida will have to work hard to prevent the python problem from getting worse.

came up with the idea to have people in the community look for pythons as they work.

Water and electric company employees and wildlife rangers have joined the Python Patrol. So have animal rescue workers, police officers, and fire fighters. They attended classes to learn how to capture the big snakes. The patrollers work in the Florida Keys, a string of islands near the southern tip of Florida. Few pythons have been found as far south as the Keys, but conservationists want to keep it that way. Like the Everglades, the Florida Keys form a delicate ecosystem. The unusual species that live on the Keys wouldn't be likely to survive the arrival of a top predator such as the python.

For the rest of the state, keeping pythons contained is nearly impossible. Forbidding the sale of pythons in the state might not work. People could still buy snakes in other states and bring them home. One suggestion is that snake owners should register their pythons. An identity chip would be inserted under the snake's skin so the owners could be traced. Similar programs are used to identify cat and dog owners. This would be an expensive plan. But it might reduce the number of snakes sold.

The state has developed an adoption program that allows people to give up unwanted snakes. The program reduces the number of snakes released in the wild, but it does not stop the problem. Even if no other pythons were discarded, the python population would continue to grow in Florida. The pythons are breeding.

It is probably too late to get rid of all the pythons in Florida's wilderness areas. The best Florida wildlife experts can do is capture as many snakes as possible. Captured pythons are killed or placed in zoos or on reptile farms. Florida's state law enforcement officers have official permission to kill any exotic reptiles they find. Pythons are the main targets. However, snakes are not found very easily, so deaths by law officers have been few.

Scientists are using some of the captured snakes to help determine python behavior in the wild. They use radio-tracking devices to map the movements of the snakes. The tagged pythons have answered a number of key questions for scientists. They have learned that pythons are now living

The more scientists learn about python behavior, the better chance they have of stopping the snakes from spreading any farther.

in all areas of the Everglades. Before the study, they thought that the snakes were sticking to areas near roads. The tracking units record the snakes' temperatures. The information helps scientists figure out where the snakes go and when the females lay eggs. This information may help scientists develop a trap for catching pythons.

LEARNING & INNOVATION SKILLS

One way to study pythons is to find out where they go. Experts knew that tracking pythons would take some creative thinking. That's where technology comes into play. Scientists have put radio transmitters in python bodies. They used the equipment to track the movements of the snakes. One snake traveled 35 miles (56.3 kilometers), while another moved 43 miles (69.2 km). Trackers collected one of the snakes when it traveled too close to a Miccosukee Indian Reservation. By acting on a clever idea, experts were able to learn more about the python's ability to travel long distances.

One Everglades wildlife technician has tried training a beagle puppy to track pythons. The idea is to train the dog to pick up a python's scent and bark when one has been found. This would help experts find and remove the snakes.

Why not introduce a predator to keep the python problem under control? This is one idea that conservationists are often quick to reject. Nature works in a balance. When humans introduce a new species to control another, the new species might become a problem. Besides, there are very few predators that will take on an adult python.

There is a lot of work to do before a plan can be developed to control the python population. Rangers want to start an in-school public education program. The goal is to get pet owners to think twice before either buying a python or releasing one into the wild. They also want laws to restrict the sale of exotic pets.

Any plan costs money. Consider the idea of a python trap. The research and development of a trap costs thousands of dollars. It would take more money to buy enough traps and pay people to maintain them and collect captured snakes. One person cannot handle an adult python. A team would be responsible for up to 20 or 30 traps. But how many traps would be enough? Where would the traps go? What would teams do with the snakes they catch?

Lawmakers are trying to reduce the number of invasive animal species that are brought into the United States. In 2009, a bill came before the U.S. Congress to ban the importation and breeding of many invasive species. The bill has the support of the Nature Conservancy and the National Audubon

Pythons will likely continue to be a problem for Florida's ecosystems for years to come.

Society, two important conservation groups. The bill would not ban all imports. It targets species that pose a serious threat to wildlife in the United States, such as Burmese pythons.

While humans are busy studying and planning, pythons are busy as well. They are eating and growing. They are producing more pythons, and finding new habitats in which to thrive. Time will tell how the struggle with these animal invaders will play out.

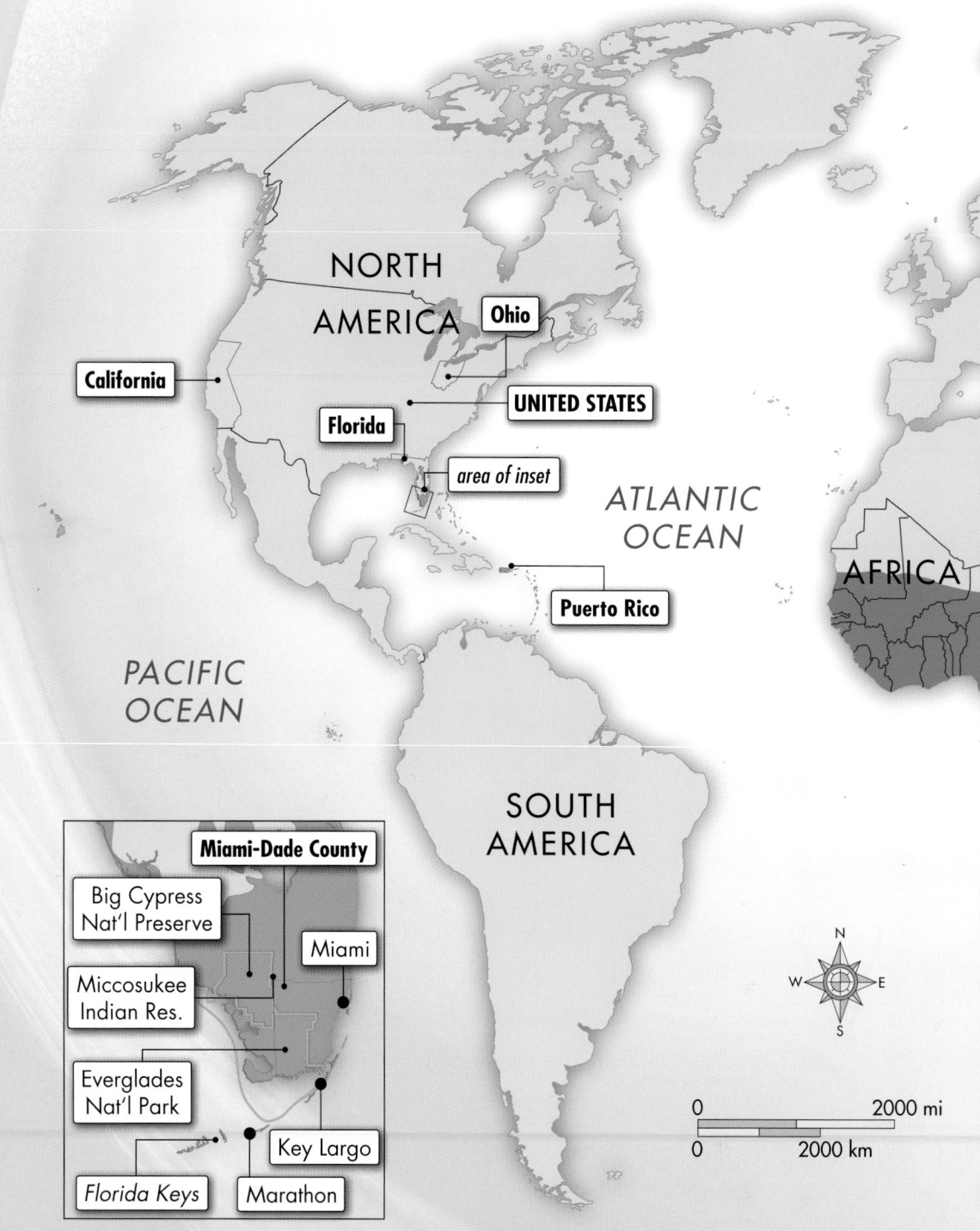

NORTH
AMERICA

Ohio

California

UNITED STATES

Florida

area of inset

ATLANTIC
OCEAN

AFRICA

Puerto Rico

PACIFIC
OCEAN

SOUTH
AMERICA

Miami-Dade County

Big Cypress
Nat'l Preserve

Miami

Miccosukee
Indian Res.

Everglades
Nat'l Park

Florida Keys

Key Largo

Marathon

N
W   E
S

0   2000 mi
0   2000 km

This map shows where in the world pythons
live naturally and where they have invaded.

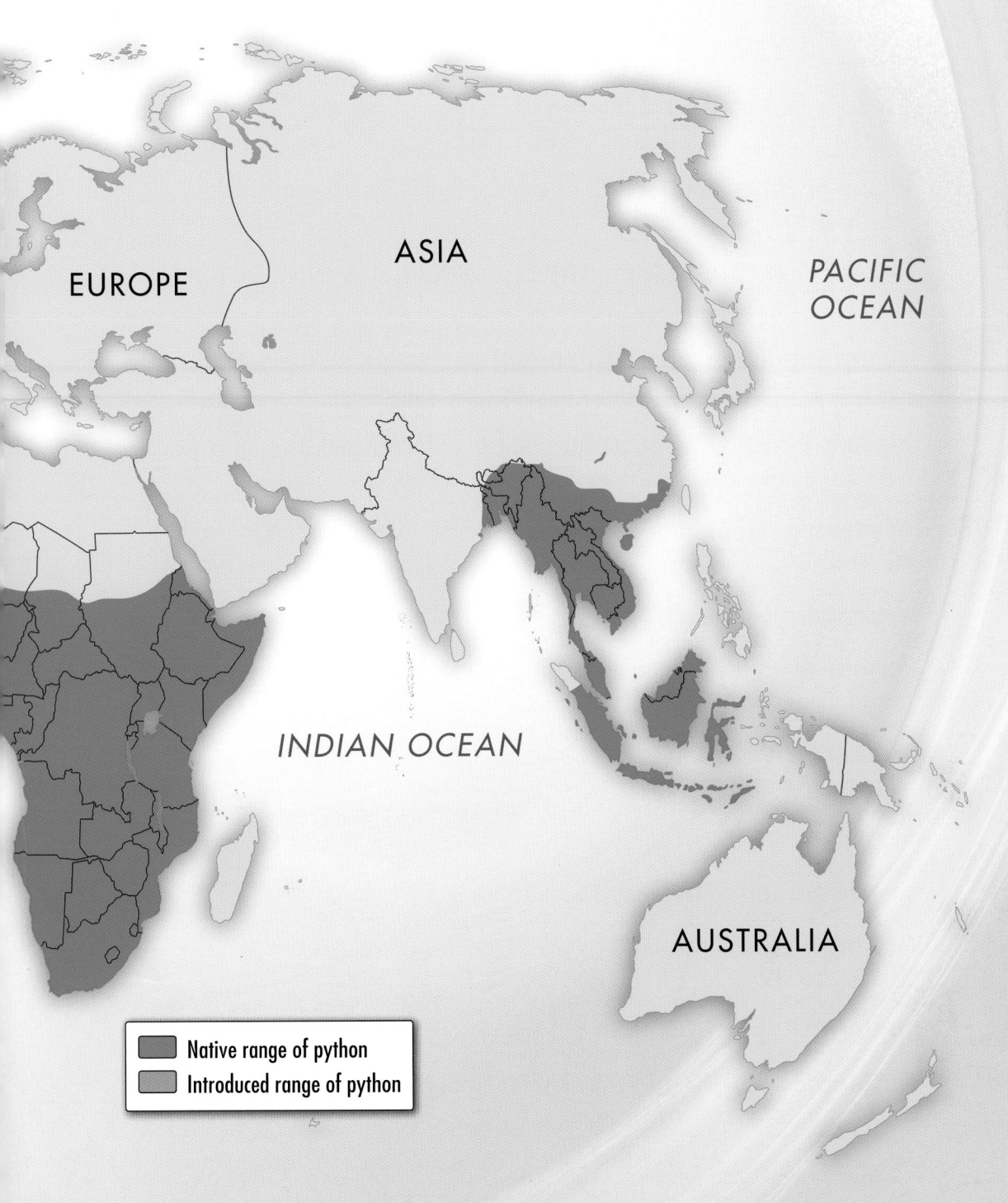

EUROPE

ASIA

PACIFIC OCEAN

INDIAN OCEAN

AUSTRALIA

Native range of python
Introduced range of python

GLOSSARY

biologist (bye-OL-uh-jist) a scientist who studies the growth and life processes of living things

camouflage (KAM-uh-flahzh) coloring that makes something look like its surroundings

conservation (kon-sur-VAY-shuhn) the preservation, management, and care of natural resources such as forests and wildlife

dissect (di-SEKT) to cut open an animal or human body to examine it

ecosystem (EE-koh-siss-tuhm) a community of plants, animals, and other organisms together with their environment, working as a unit

endangered (en-DAYN-jurd) at risk of dying out completely

feral (FIHR-uhl) relating to a wild animal or describing a domestic animal that has returned to the wild

habitat (HAB-uh-tat) the area where plants or animals normally live

invasive species (in-VAY-siv SPEE-sheez) any plants or animals that are not native to an area but have moved into the region

nocturnal (nok-TUR-nuhl) active at night

predator (PRED-uh-tur) an animal that hunts and kills other animals for food

prey (PRAY) an animal that is hunted by another for food

suffocates (SUHF-uh-kaytss) dies from lack of air or oxygen or from not being allowed to breathe

FOR MORE INFORMATION

BOOKS

Fiedler, Julie. *Pythons*. New York: PowerKids Press, 2008.

Higgins, Nadia. *Welcome to Everglades National Park*. Chanhassen, MN: Child's World, 2007.

Rothaus, Don. *Pythons*. Chanhassen, MN: Child's World, 2007.

WEB SITES

National Geographic Kids—Python Pete
kids.nationalgeographic.com/Photos/DogsJobs/Python-pete?vgnextfmt=enlarge
Find a photo and information about a dog used to help track down pythons.

National Zoological Park—Burmese Python
nationalzoo.si.edu/Animals/ReptilesAmphibians/Exhibit/Profiles/default.cfm?id=41
Get more information on Burmese pythons.

San Diego Zoo—Reptiles: Python
www.sandiegozoo.org/animalbytes/t-python.html
Learn more about pythons, and hear what they sound like through a brief audio clip.

INDEX

ABOUT THE AUTHOR

Barbara Somervill writes children's nonfiction books on a variety of topics. Because she lived in Australia, where animal invaders abound, she finds investigating these "imported accidents" fascinating. Barbara takes conservation issues seriously. She is an avid recycler and an active member of several conservation organizations.